I0479789

Passive Income Power Play:

How to Build Wealth and Retire Aggressively.

by

Alan S. Rodriguez

I. Introduction

This book is designed to help you understand the power of passive income and how it can transform your financial future. Whether you are a beginner or an experienced investor, this book will provide you with valuable insights and practical strategies for building a portfolio of passive income streams that can generate wealth and support your retirement goals.

In today's world, traditional employment is becoming less secure and reliable as the economy changes rapidly. To achieve financial freedom, exploring new and innovative ways of generating income that doesn't rely on traditional jobs is essential. Passive income is the key to achieving financial independence and retiring aggressively, and this book will show you how to make it work for you.

This book will explore different types of passive income opportunities, including real estate, stocks, and alternative investments. You will learn how to create a plan for building your passive income portfolio, assess your financial situation and resources, and identify the best opportunities for maximizing your returns.

By the end of this book, you will have a clear understanding of the power of passive income and how to harness it for your financial benefit. You will be equipped with practical strategies and tools for building a diversified portfolio of passive income streams that can support your lifestyle goals and help you achieve true financial independence. Let's get started!

Overall, this book will equip you with the knowledge, skills, and tools you need to build a diversified portfolio of passive income streams that can support your financial goals and provide you with long-term financial security and stability.

II. Understanding Passive Income

Passive income refers to income that is earned without active involvement or effort. It is often contrasted with active income, which is income earned through work or employment.

Passive income streams can come from a variety of sources, including investments, business ventures, and real estate. Some examples of passive income streams include rental income from real estate, dividend income from stocks, interest income from bonds or savings accounts, and royalties from intellectual property.

The main benefit of passive income is that it allows you to earn money without having to trade your time for it. This means that you can continue to generate income even while you're not actively working, giving you more freedom and flexibility to pursue other interests or spend time with your family.

Moreover, passive income can help you achieve financial independence and retire early because it can provide a steady stream of income that can support your lifestyle needs without having to rely on traditional employment.

By building a portfolio of passive income streams, you can diversify your income sources and reduce your dependence on a single source of income.

Overall, passive income is a powerful tool for building long-term financial security and stability. By understanding the different types of passive income opportunities and how to create a diversified portfolio of income streams, you can take control of your financial future and achieve your financial goals.

What is passive income and how does it differ from active income?

Passive income is income earned without requiring active involvement or effort on your part. This type of income often comes from investments, real estate, or other sources that generate ongoing revenue streams. Examples of passive income include rental income, dividend income from stocks, interest income from savings accounts, and royalties from intellectual property.

Active income, on the other hand, is earned through work or employment. This type of income typically requires you to trade your time and effort for compensation.

Examples of active income include salaries, wages, and commissions earned from a job or business.

The key difference between passive and active income is that passive income allows you to earn money without the need for active participation or direct effort. This means that passive income streams can continue to generate income even when you're not actively working. In contrast, active income requires ongoing work and effort to maintain your income stream.

Passive income is often seen as a powerful tool for achieving financial independence and retiring early, as it can provide a steady stream of income that does not depend on traditional employment or active work. By building a diversified portfolio of passive income streams, you can create a reliable source of income that can support your financial goals and provide you with greater financial freedom and flexibility.

The benefits of passive income over traditional employment

Passive income has several benefits over traditional employment, including:

1. Flexibility: Passive income streams often require less time and effort than traditional employment, allowing you to have greater flexibility in how you spend your time. You can often work from anywhere, at any time, and don't have to stick to a set schedule or routine.

2. Freedom: With passive income, you're not tied to a specific job or employer, giving you greater freedom to pursue your interests and hobbies. You can also choose to work on projects that you're passionate about, rather than simply doing work for a paycheck.

3. Diversification: Passive income streams can come from a variety of sources, including real estate, investments, and royalties. This allows you to diversify your income and reduce your dependence on a single source of income.

4. Scalability: Passive income streams can often be scaled up or down depending on your needs and goals. For example, you can increase your rental income by buying additional properties or expand your investment portfolio to increase your dividend income.

5. Security: Passive income can provide a reliable source of income that is not dependent on traditional

employment or the ups and downs of the job market. This can provide greater financial security and stability in the long run.

Overall, passive income offers many benefits over traditional employment, including greater flexibility, freedom, diversification, scalability, and security. By building a diversified portfolio of passive income streams, you can create a reliable source of income that can support your financial goals and provide you with greater financial freedom and flexibility.

Types of passive income streams and their characteristics

Passive income streams can come from various sources, and each type of passive income stream has its own unique characteristics. Here are some examples of passive income streams and their characteristics:

1. Rental Income: Rental income is earned by owning and renting out real estate properties. Rental income is a reliable source of passive income that can provide a steady stream of cash flow over time. However, it requires significant upfront investment and ongoing maintenance costs.

2. Dividend Income: Dividend income is earned by investing in dividend-paying stocks. Dividend income can provide a regular source of income that can be reinvested to grow your portfolio. However, it is subject to fluctuations in the stock market, and dividends can be cut or eliminated by companies at any time.

3. Interest Income: Interest income is earned by investing in bonds or savings accounts. Interest income is a low-risk source of passive income that can provide a predictable return on investment. However, interest rates are often low, and inflation can erode the value of your returns over time.

4. Royalties: Royalties are earned by owning and licensing intellectual property, such as books, music, or software. Royalties can provide a significant source of passive income with little to no ongoing maintenance required. However, creating intellectual property can require significant upfront investment and may not generate reliable income over time.

5. Business Ownership: Passive income can also be earned by owning a business and hiring others to manage it. Business ownership can provide a significant source of income with the potential for

growth and expansion. However, owning a business can be risky and requires ongoing management and oversight.

Overall, each type of passive income stream has its own unique characteristics, advantages, and disadvantages. By diversifying your passive income streams, you can create a reliable source of income that can support your financial goals and provide you with greater financial freedom and flexibility.

III. Building Your Passive Income Portfolio

Building a passive income portfolio requires careful planning and execution. Here are some steps you can take to build your passive income portfolio:

1. Set Your Goals: The first step in building a passive income portfolio is to define your financial goals. Consider how much passive income you need to achieve financial independence, retire early, or achieve other financial goals.

2. Identify Income Streams: Once you have your goals in mind, the next step is to identify potential sources of passive income. Consider your existing assets, such as real estate, stocks, or other investments, and explore new opportunities, such as creating intellectual property or starting a business.

3. Evaluate Risks and Rewards: Before investing in any passive income stream, evaluate the risks and rewards associated with it. Consider factors such as the potential return on investment, ongoing maintenance costs, and the level of risk involved.

4. Diversify Your Portfolio: Diversifying your passive income portfolio is critical to reduce risk and increase potential returns. Consider investing in a variety of

passive income streams to spread your risk and create a reliable source of income.

5. Monitor Your Portfolio: Once you have built your passive income portfolio, it's important to monitor it regularly to ensure that it continues to meet your financial goals. Evaluate the performance of each income stream and make adjustments as needed to maximize your returns and minimize risk.

By following these steps and continuously building and diversifying your passive income portfolio, you can create a reliable source of income that can support your financial goals and provide you with greater financial freedom and flexibility.

Identifying your financial goals and creating a plan

Identifying your financial goals and creating a plan is a critical first step in building a passive income portfolio. Here are some steps you can take to identify your financial goals and create a plan:

1. Define Your Financial Goals: Start by identifying your financial goals, such as retiring early, achieving financial independence, or saving for a down

payment on a home. Make sure your goals are specific, measurable, and realistic

2. Assess Your Current Finances: Once you have identified your financial goals, assess your current finances to determine where you stand. Calculate your net worth, evaluate your income and expenses, and determine how much you can save each month.

3. Determine Your Passive Income Needs: Consider how much passive income you need to achieve your financial goals. Calculate your current expenses, and determine how much passive income you need to cover those expenses.

4. Identify Potential Passive Income Streams: Identify potential sources of passive income based on your financial goals and needs. Consider your existing assets, such as real estate or investments, and explore new opportunities, such as creating intellectual property or starting a business.

5. Create a Plan: Develop a plan to achieve your financial goals by building a passive income portfolio. Set milestones and create a timeline for achieving your goals. Determine how much you need to invest and what income streams you need to pursue to achieve your goals.

6. Monitor Your Progress: Once you have created a plan, monitor your progress regularly to ensure that you are on track to achieving your financial goals. Evaluate your passive income streams and adjust your plan as needed to maximize your returns and minimize risk.

By identifying your financial goals and creating a plan, you can build a passive income portfolio that supports your financial goals and provides you with greater financial freedom and flexibility.

Assessing your current financial situation and resources

Assessing your current financial situation and resources is an essential step in building a passive income portfolio. Here are some steps you can take to assess your current financial situation and resources:

1. Calculate Your Net Worth: Your net worth is your assets minus your liabilities. Calculate your net worth by listing all your assets, such as your savings, investments, and real estate, and subtracting all your liabilities, such as your loans and credit card debt.

2. Evaluate Your Income and Expenses: Evaluate your income and expenses to determine how much money you have coming in and going out each month. Create a budget to track your expenses and determine where you can cut costs.

3. Determine Your Savings Rate: Your savings rate is the percentage of your income that you save each month. Determine your savings rate by dividing your monthly savings by your monthly income.

4. Evaluate Your Assets: Evaluate your existing assets, such as real estate, investments, and intellectual property, to determine their potential as a source of passive income. Consider how much income they can generate, how much maintenance they require, and any associated costs.

5. Consider Your Liabilities: Consider your liabilities, such as loans and credit card debt, and how they impact your ability to invest in passive income streams. Determine how much you can afford to invest each month while still meeting your financial obligations.

6. Identify Opportunities for Passive Income: Identify potential sources of passive income based on your financial situation and resources. Consider starting a

side hustle, investing in real estate or stocks, or creating intellectual property.

By assessing your current financial situation and resources, you can determine how much you can invest in passive income streams and identify opportunities that align with your financial goals. This can help you build a passive income portfolio that provides you with greater financial freedom and flexibility.

Evaluating and selecting passive income opportunities
Evaluating and selecting passive income opportunities requires careful consideration of several factors. Here are some steps you can take to evaluate and select passive income opportunities:

1. Determine Your Investment Criteria: Determine your investment criteria based on your financial goals and risk tolerance. Consider factors such as return on investment, risk level, liquidity, and time horizon.
2. Research Opportunities: Research potential passive income opportunities based on your investment criteria. Consider real estate investment trusts (REITs), dividend-paying stocks, peer-to-peer

lending, rental properties, or creating intellectual property.

3. Evaluate the Opportunity: Evaluate the potential opportunity based on factors such as the rate of return, fees and expenses, risk level, and liquidity. Compare the opportunity to similar investments to determine its relative value.

4. Assess the Risks: Assess the risks associated with the opportunity, such as market volatility, inflation, and interest rate risk. Consider the potential impact of these risks on your investment returns.

5. Consider the Investment Horizon: Consider the investment horizon for the opportunity, such as short-term or long-term. Determine if the opportunity aligns with your investment goals and time horizon.

6. Seek Professional Advice: Seek professional advice from financial advisors or other experts to evaluate the opportunity and determine its potential benefits and risks.

By evaluating and selecting passive income opportunities carefully, you can build a diversified passive income portfolio that generates consistent and reliable income while minimizing risk. This can help you achieve your financial goals and provide you with greater financial freedom and flexibility.

Diversifying your income streams for maximum stability

Diversifying your income streams is a key strategy for achieving maximum stability in your passive income portfolio. Here are some steps you can take to diversify your income streams:

1. Invest in Different Asset Classes: Invest in different asset classes, such as real estate, stocks, bonds, and commodities. Diversifying across asset classes can help reduce the overall risk in your portfolio and provide more stable returns over time

2. Consider Different Industries: Consider investing in different industries, such as technology, healthcare, or consumer goods. This can help diversify your portfolio and reduce the impact of industry-specific risks.

3. Explore Different Types of Passive Income Opportunities: Explore different types of passive income opportunities, such as rental income, dividend income, interest income, or royalty income. By investing in a variety of income streams, you can

reduce the overall risk in your portfolio and generate more stable returns over time

4. Utilize Different Investment Vehicles: Utilize different investment vehicles, such as mutual funds, exchange-traded funds (ETFs), or real estate investment trusts (REITs). This can help diversify your portfolio and reduce the impact of individual stock or property risks.

5. Monitor and Adjust Your Portfolio: Regularly monitor and adjust your portfolio to ensure that it remains diversified and aligned with your investment goals. Rebalance your portfolio periodically to ensure that your investments remain diversified and aligned with your financial goals.

By diversifying your income streams, you can build a more stable and reliable passive income portfolio that generates consistent income over time. This can help you achieve your financial goals and provide you with greater financial freedom and flexibility.

IV. Real Estate Investing for Passive Income

Real estate investing can be a powerful way to generate passive income. Here are some steps you can take to invest in real estate for passive income:

1. Determine Your Investment Criteria: Determine your investment criteria based on your financial goals and risk tolerance. Consider factors such as return on investment, risk level, liquidity, and time horizon.
2. Choose a Real Estate Investment Strategy: Choose a real estate investment strategy that aligns with your investment criteria, such as rental properties, real estate crowdfunding, or real estate investment trusts (REITs).
3. Evaluate Properties: Evaluate potential properties based on factors such as location, condition, and rental income potential. Consider working with a real estate agent or property manager to help identify suitable properties.
4. Secure Financing: Secure financing for your real estate investment through traditional mortgage lenders, private lenders, or crowdfunding platforms.
5. Manage Your Investment: Once you have acquired a property, manage it effectively to generate passive

income. This may involve finding suitable tenants, maintaining the property, and handling any tenant issues or maintenance needs that arise.

6. Monitor and Adjust Your Portfolio: Regularly monitor and adjust your real estate portfolio to ensure that it remains diversified and aligned with your investment goals. Rebalance your portfolio periodically to ensure that your investments remain diversified and aligned with your financial goals.

By investing in real estate for passive income, you can generate consistent income over time and build a diversified portfolio that is less susceptible to market volatility. With careful research and management, real estate investing can be an effective way to achieve your financial goals and provide you with greater financial freedom and flexibility.

Benefits and risks of real estate investing

Real estate investing can offer several benefits and risks, depending on your investment strategy and the specific properties you choose. Here are some of the key benefits and risks of real estate investing:

A. Benefits:

1. Passive Income: Real estate investing can generate passive income through rental income, providing a consistent stream of cash flow over time.

2. Appreciation: Over time, real estate can appreciate in value, which can increase the overall return on your investment.

3. Tax Benefits: Real estate investors can take advantage of tax benefits such as depreciation deductions and write-offs for expenses related to the property.

4. Diversification: Real estate investing can provide diversification in a portfolio, reducing the overall risk and increasing the potential return.

5. Control: Real estate investors have a high degree of control over their investment, including the ability to make decisions about property management, renovations, and rental rates.

B. Risks:

1. Market Volatility: Real estate markets can be volatile, and property values can fluctuate based on factors such as interest rates, local economic conditions, and demographic changes.

2. Property Management: Managing a rental property can be time-consuming and expensive, requiring ongoing maintenance and dealing with tenant issues.

3. Cash Flow Risks: Rental income can be unpredictable, and there is a risk that rental income may not cover expenses such as mortgage payments, taxes, and maintenance costs.

4. Liquidity Risks: Real estate investments are relatively illiquid, meaning that they cannot be easily sold or converted into cash.

5. Legal Risks: Real estate investing involves legal risks, such as liability for accidents or injuries on the property, zoning restrictions, and landlord-tenant laws.

Before investing in real estate, it is important to carefully evaluate your investment goals, risk tolerance, and the specific properties you are considering. Working with a real estate professional or financial advisor can help you make informed investment decisions and manage risks effectively.

Types of real estate investments and their potential returns

There are several types of real estate investments that can offer potential returns, depending on your investment strategy and the specific properties you choose. Here are some of the most common types of real estate investments and their potential returns:

1. Rental Properties: Rental properties are one of the most popular types of real estate investments. Investors purchase a property and rent it out to tenants, generating rental income that can provide a steady stream of cash flow. The potential return on a rental property can vary depending on factors such as the rental rates, occupancy rate, and property expenses. Rental properties can offer a potential return of 6% to 12% annually.

2. Real Estate Investment Trusts (REITs): A REIT is a company that owns or finances income-producing real estate. Investors can buy shares in a REIT, which provides exposure to the real estate market without having to purchase and manage properties directly. REITs can offer a potential return of 5% to 10% annually.

3. Flipping Properties: Flipping properties involves purchasing a property, renovating it, and then selling it for a profit. The potential return on a flipped property can vary depending on the purchase price, renovation costs, and sale price. Flipping properties can offer a potential return of 10% to 20% annually.

4. Real Estate Crowdfunding: Real estate crowdfunding involves pooling funds from multiple investors to purchase or finance a property. Investors can invest in specific properties or portfolios of properties, and receive a portion of the rental income or profits. The potential return on real estate crowdfunding can vary depending on the specific investment and the level of risk. Real estate crowdfunding can offer a potential return of 8% to 12% annually.

5. Commercial Properties: Commercial properties include office buildings, retail centers, and industrial properties. These properties can generate rental income from tenants, and can offer a potential return of 6% to 12% annually.

When investing in real estate, it is important to carefully evaluate the potential risks and rewards of each investment type, and to choose a strategy that aligns with your investment goals and risk tolerance. Working with a real estate professional or financial advisor can help you make informed investment decisions and maximize your potential returns.

Strategies for acquiring and managing rental properties

Acquiring and managing rental properties can be a complex and challenging process, but there are several strategies that can help you be successful. Here are some strategies for acquiring and managing rental properties:

1. Research the market: Before purchasing a rental property, it is important to research the local real estate market to determine the potential rental income and demand. Look for properties in areas with a strong rental market, such as near universities, public transportation, or job centers.

2. Analyze the financials: Analyze the financials of a potential rental property to ensure that it is a good investment. Consider the purchase price, rental income, expenses (including property taxes, insurance, and maintenance costs), and potential vacancy rates. Make sure that the rental income will cover the expenses and provide a positive cash flow.

3. Screen tenants: Tenant screening is an important part of managing rental properties. Screen potential tenants carefully, checking their credit history, rental history, and income. Choose tenants who are reliable, responsible, and able to pay rent on time.

4. Maintain the property: Keeping a rental property in good condition is important for attracting and retaining tenants. Regularly inspect the property and make necessary repairs and upgrades. Respond promptly to tenant maintenance requests and keep the property clean and well-maintained.

5. Use property management services: Property management services can help you manage your rental properties more effectively, handling tasks such as tenant screening, rent collection, maintenance, and repairs. Hiring a property management company can save you time and stress, but it will also come at a cost.

6. Set rental rates appropriately: Setting the rental rate too high can lead to longer vacancy periods, while setting the rental rate too low can reduce your potential rental income. Research the local market to set rental rates appropriately.

7. Create a lease agreement: A lease agreement is a legally binding contract between the landlord and tenant that outlines the terms of the rental agreement. Make sure that the lease agreement is clear, comprehensive, and compliant with local laws.

By following these strategies, you can increase your chances of success in acquiring and managing rental properties. It is also important to stay up-to-date with local real estate market trends and regulations, and to work with a real estate professional or financial advisor to make informed investment decisions.

Maximizing profits through real estate syndication and crowdfunding

Real estate syndication and crowdfunding are two popular strategies for maximizing profits through real estate investing. Here's how each of these strategies work:

A. Real Estate Syndication

Real estate syndication involves pooling together resources from multiple investors to purchase a property. The investors, known as limited partners, provide the capital while a sponsor, known as a general partner, manages the property and the investment. The sponsor typically takes a percentage of the profits as a fee for their services.

The benefits of real estate syndication include the ability to invest in larger properties with higher potential returns, access to the expertise of the sponsor, and the potential for passive income. However, real estate syndication can be complex and involves legal and regulatory requirements that must be followed.

B. Real Estate Crowdfunding:

Real estate crowdfunding is a relatively new strategy that allows investors to pool together smaller amounts of capital to invest in real estate projects. Crowdfunding platforms typically offer investors access to a range of projects with varying investment minimums.

The benefits of real estate crowdfunding include the ability to invest in a diverse range of properties and projects, lower investment minimums, and the potential for passive income. However, real estate crowdfunding can also involve higher fees and lower potential returns than traditional real estate investing. To maximize profits through real estate syndication and crowdfunding, it is important to research and choose reputable sponsors and crowdfunding platforms, evaluate the potential returns and risks of each investment opportunity, and diversify your portfolio across a range of properties and projects. It is also important to work with a financial advisor or real estate professional to make informed investment decisions.

V. Stock Market Investing for Passive Income

Investing in the stock market can be a great way to generate passive income. Here are some strategies for investing in the stock market for passive income:

1. Dividend Investing: Dividend investing involves investing in stocks that pay dividends, which are regular payments made by companies to their shareholders. Dividend investing can provide a reliable stream of passive income, as long as the companies continue to pay dividends.

2. Growth Stocks: Investing in growth stocks can also provide passive income in the form of capital gains. Growth stocks are stocks of companies that are expected to grow at a faster rate than the overall market. As the stock price of these companies increases, investors can sell their shares for a profit.

3. Index Funds: Investing in index funds can be a passive way to invest in the stock market. Index funds are funds that track a particular stock market index, such as the S&P 500. By investing in an index fund, investors can gain exposure to a diverse range of stocks and benefit from the overall performance of the market.

4. Exchange-Traded Funds (ETFs): ETFs are similar to index funds in that they track a particular index, but they are traded like individual stocks. ETFs can be a passive way to invest in a particular sector or market index.

5. Robo-Advisors: Robo-advisors are digital platforms that use algorithms to automatically manage and invest money. Robo-advisors can provide a low-cost and passive way to invest in the stock market, as they handle all investment decisions and rebalancing.

To maximize profits through stock market investing, it is important to diversify your portfolio across a range of stocks and investments, regularly evaluate your investments, and work with a financial advisor or investment professional to make informed investment decisions. It is also important to understand the potential risks and volatility of the stock market and to have a long-term investment strategy.

The power of dividends and how they work

Dividends are a portion of a company's profits that are distributed to its shareholders on a regular basis, typically quarterly. Dividends can be paid in the form of cash or additional shares of stock. Dividend payments are typically decided by a company's board of directors and are announced on a regular schedule.

Dividend payments can be a powerful tool for generating passive income, as they provide a regular stream of income without requiring the investor to sell their shares. Dividend payments can also provide a measure of stability in a volatile market, as companies that pay dividends typically have a proven track record of profitability and financial stability.

Dividend payments are typically classified as either qualified or non-qualified dividends. Qualified dividends are subject to a lower tax rate than non-qualified dividends, making them a more tax-efficient source of passive income. In order to qualify for the lower tax rate, the dividends must be paid by a U.S. corporation or a qualifying foreign corporation and held for a certain period of time.

It's important to note that not all companies pay dividends, and the amount and frequency of dividend payments can vary widely between companies. Investors should carefully research a company's dividend history and financial stability before investing in their stock for dividend income.

Overall, dividends can be a powerful tool for generating passive income and building long-term wealth through the stock market. By investing in companies with a track record of regular dividend payments and financial stability, investors can benefit from a reliable stream of income and potential capital gains over time.

Choosing dividend-paying stocks and funds

When choosing dividend-paying stocks and funds, there are a few key factors to consider:

1. Dividend Yield: The dividend yield is the annual dividend payment divided by the current stock price. A higher dividend yield can indicate a higher potential return on investment, but it's important to evaluate the company's financial health and stability before investing.

2. Dividend History: A company's history of paying dividends can be a good indicator of its financial stability and long-term potential for generating passive income. Look for companies with a

consistent track record of paying dividends over several years.

3. Financial Health: It's important to evaluate the financial health of the company or fund before investing in its stock. Look at factors such as revenue growth, earnings per share, debt levels, and cash flow to ensure that the company or fund is financially stable and capable of continuing to pay dividends.

4. Diversification: Diversifying your dividend portfolio across multiple companies and sectors can help to reduce risk and increase potential returns. Consider investing in a mix of large-cap and small-cap stocks, as well as stocks from different industries.

5. Tax Efficiency: Qualified dividends are subject to a lower tax rate than non-qualified dividends. Consider investing in stocks and funds that pay qualified dividends to minimize your tax liability.

When choosing dividend-paying stocks and funds, it can be helpful to work with a financial advisor or investment professional to make informed investment decisions. By carefully evaluating the potential risks and returns of each investment and building a diversified portfolio, investors can maximize their potential for generating passive income through dividend payments.

Understanding stock market trends and risk management

Understanding stock market trends and risk management is crucial for passive income investors in the stock market. Here are some key concepts to consider:

1. Market Trends: The stock market can be volatile, and it's important to understand market trends in order to make informed investment decisions. Look at factors such as historical performance, economic indicators, and market news to identify trends and potential opportunities for growth.

2. Risk Management: All investments carry a certain degree of risk, and it's important to manage risk in order to protect your investments and generate consistent passive income. Consider factors such as diversification, asset allocation, and stop-loss orders to help manage risk and protect your investments.

3. Portfolio Rebalancing: Over time, your investment portfolio may become unbalanced due to changes in market conditions or individual stock performance. Regularly rebalancing your portfolio can help to ensure that your investments are aligned with your long-term financial goals and risk tolerance.

4. Investment Strategies: There are a variety of investment strategies that can be used to generate passive income in the stock market, such as dividend investing, growth investing, and value investing. Consider your financial goals, risk tolerance, and investment timeframe when choosing an investment strategy.

5. Long-Term Perspective: Passive income investing in the stock market requires a long-term perspective and patience. It's important to avoid making emotional investment decisions based on short-term market fluctuations and to stay focused on your long-term financial goals.

By understanding market trends and managing risk, passive income investors in the stock market can maximize their potential for generating consistent income and building long-term wealth. It's important to work with a financial advisor or investment professional to develop an investment strategy that aligns with your financial goals and risk tolerance.

Tax implications and strategies for optimizing returns

Passive income from investments, including real estate and the stock market, is generally subject to taxes. Understanding the tax implications and implementing strategies to optimize returns can help passive income investors maximize their profits. Here are some tax-related concepts and strategies to consider:

1. Taxation of Passive Income: Passive income from investments is generally subject to federal and state income taxes, as well as capital gains taxes. The tax rates vary depending on the type of investment and the length of time it is held. It's important to understand the tax implications of each investment and factor them into your investment strategy.

2. Tax-Advantaged Accounts: Certain investment accounts, such as Individual Retirement Accounts (IRAs) and 401(k) plans, offer tax advantages that can help to reduce your tax liability and optimize your returns. Contributions to these accounts may be tax-deductible, and investment gains may be tax-deferred or tax-free.

3. Tax-Loss Harvesting: Tax-loss harvesting involves selling losing investments in order to offset gains and reduce your tax liability. This strategy can be used to

optimize your returns and reduce your overall tax burden.

4. Depreciation and Deductions: Real estate investors can take advantage of tax deductions and depreciation to reduce their tax liability and optimize their returns. Deductions may include expenses such as property taxes, mortgage interest, and maintenance costs, while depreciation allows investors to deduct a portion of the cost of the property over time.

5. Estate Planning: Estate planning can help to minimize the tax burden on your investments and ensure that your assets are distributed according to your wishes. Strategies such as gifting, trusts, and charitable donations can help to reduce estate taxes and preserve your wealth for future generations.

By understanding the tax implications of passive income investments and implementing strategies to optimize returns, investors can maximize their profits and build long-term wealth. It's important to work with a tax professional or financial advisor to develop a tax strategy that aligns with your financial goals and risk tolerance.

VI. Alternative Investments for Passive Income

In addition to real estate and the stock market, there are many other alternative investment opportunities that can generate passive income. Here are a few examples:

1. Peer-to-Peer Lending: Peer-to-peer (P2P) lending platforms allow individuals to lend money to others in exchange for interest payments. P2P lending can be a high-yield investment, but it also comes with risks such as borrower default.

2. Royalties: Royalties are payments made to the owner of a patent, copyright, or other intellectual property. Royalty payments can be a source of passive income for the owner of the intellectual property.

3. Commodities: Commodities such as gold, silver, and oil can be invested in through exchange-traded funds (ETFs) or mutual funds. These investments can generate passive income through price appreciation and dividend payments.

4. Business Investment: Investing in a small business can generate passive income through a share of the profits. However, this type of investment comes with risks and requires due diligence to ensure the viability of the business.

5. Annuities: Annuities are financial products that provide regular payments over a set period of time. Annuities can be purchased from insurance companies and can be a source of passive income during retirement.

6. Cryptocurrency: Cryptocurrency such as Bitcoin and Ethereum can be invested in through trading platforms or investment funds. While cryptocurrency can be a high-risk investment, it also has the potential for high returns.

When considering alternative investments for passive income, it's important to do your research and assess the risks and potential returns. Working with a financial advisor can help you develop a diversified investment portfolio that aligns with your financial goals and risk tolerance.

Introduction to alternative investments and their potential benefits

Alternative investments are investment options that go beyond traditional stocks, bonds, and cash. These investments can provide opportunities for diversification, the potential for higher returns, and passive income generation. Here are some potential benefits of alternative investments:

1. Diversification: Alternative investments can offer diversification beyond traditional stocks and bonds. This can help reduce risk and provide a more balanced investment portfolio.
2. Potential for higher returns: Some alternative investments, such as private equity or real estate, can provide higher returns than traditional investments. However, these investments often come with higher risks.
3. Passive income generation: Many alternative investments, such as real estate, can provide a stream of passive income through rental payments or dividend payments.
4. Hedge against inflation: Some alternative investments, such as commodities, can provide a hedge against inflation by potentially increasing in value as the cost of living rises.
5. Non-correlated returns: Alternative investments often have returns that are not correlated with traditional investments, which means they can perform well even when traditional investments are struggling.

It's important to note that alternative investments can come with higher risks and fees compared to traditional investments. It's important to do your due diligence and work with a financial advisor to ensure that these investments align with your financial goals and risk tolerance.

Investing in bonds, commodities, and precious metals
Investing in bonds, commodities, and precious metals are examples of alternative investments that can provide diversification and potential returns. Here's a closer look at each of these options:

1. Bonds: Bonds are a type of fixed income investment that can provide regular interest payments and potentially higher returns than traditional savings accounts. Bonds can be issued by corporations, municipalities, or the government, and come in a variety of forms such as Treasury bonds or corporate bonds. Investing in bonds can provide diversification and stability to an investment portfolio, but they do come with risks such as interest rate changes and credit risk.

2. Commodities: Commodities are tangible goods such as gold, silver, oil, or agricultural products that can be traded on commodity markets. Investing in commodities can provide diversification and potential for returns based on global supply and demand. However, investing in commodities can also be volatile and subject to fluctuations in prices due to geopolitical events or natural disasters.

3. Precious Metals: Precious metals such as gold and silver have been used as a store of value for centuries. Investing in precious metals can provide diversification and a hedge against inflation. Precious metals can be purchased as physical bullion or through exchange-traded funds (ETFs). However, investing in precious metals can also be volatile and subject to fluctuations in supply and demand.

When investing in alternative investments such as bonds, commodities, and precious metals, it's important to understand the risks and potential returns. Working with a financial advisor can help you determine if these investments align with your financial goals and risk tolerance.

Peer-to-peer lending and cryptocurrency investing

Peer-to-peer (P2P) lending and cryptocurrency investing are two additional examples of alternative investments that can provide diversification and potential returns:

1. Peer-to-Peer Lending: P2P lending is a type of lending that allows individuals to lend money directly to borrowers through an online platform, bypassing traditional banks. P2P lending can provide higher returns than traditional savings accounts or bonds, but it does come with risks such as credit risk and borrower default. It's important to carefully evaluate the platform's policies and loan quality before investing in P2P lending.

2. Cryptocurrency: Cryptocurrencies, such as Bitcoin or Ethereum, are a type of digital currency that operates independently of a central bank. Cryptocurrency can provide potential for high returns, but it is also highly volatile and subject to regulation and security risks. Investing in cryptocurrency requires a deep understanding of blockchain technology and market trends.

As with any alternative investment, it's important to do your due diligence and work with a financial advisor to ensure that P2P lending or cryptocurrency aligns with your financial goals and risk tolerance.

Pros and cons of alternative investments for passive income

Alternative investments, such as real estate, bonds, commodities, precious metals, P2P lending, and cryptocurrency, can provide diversification and potential returns for a passive income portfolio. Here are some pros and cons to consider when investing in alternative investments:

Pros:

1. Diversification: Alternative investments can provide diversification, which can help reduce overall risk in a portfolio.
2. Potential for higher returns: Alternative investments can offer higher returns than traditional investments such as stocks and bonds.
3. Hedge against inflation: Some alternative investments, such as precious metals and real estate, can act as a hedge against inflation and protect against the erosion of purchasing power.

Cons

1. Lack of liquidity: Alternative investments can be less liquid than traditional investments, meaning it may be difficult to sell them quickly or at a fair price.
2. Higher risk: Alternative investments can be riskier than traditional investments, and may require a deeper understanding of the market and investment structure.
3. Regulation and security risks: Some alternative investments, such as cryptocurrency and P2P lending, are subject to regulatory and security risks that may affect their performance and value.
4. Higher fees: Alternative investments may come with higher fees than traditional investments, such as management fees or transaction costs.

As with any investment, it's important to carefully evaluate the risks and potential rewards of alternative investments, and to work with a financial advisor to ensure that they align with your financial goals and risk tolerance.

VII. Maximizing Your Passive Income Potential

Maximizing your passive income potential requires careful planning and ongoing management. Here are some strategies to consider:

1. Reinvesting dividends: If you're investing in dividend-paying stocks or funds, consider reinvesting the dividends to maximize your returns over time.
2. Continuously evaluate and adjust your portfolio: Regularly evaluate your passive income portfolio to ensure that it aligns with your financial goals and risk tolerance. Adjust your investments as necessary to optimize your returns and manage risk.
3. Increase your investment contributions: The more you invest, the greater your potential returns. Consider increasing your contributions over time to maximize your passive income potential.
4. Expand your passive income streams: Diversify your passive income streams by investing in different types of assets, such as real estate, stocks, bonds, or P2P lending. This can help reduce risk and increase potential returns.
5. Utilize tax-efficient strategies: Consult with a tax advisor to understand tax-efficient strategies that can

help minimize taxes and maximize your after-tax returns.

6. Consider hiring a financial advisor: A financial advisor can help you develop and manage a passive income portfolio that aligns with your financial goals and risk tolerance. They can also provide guidance on tax-efficient strategies, portfolio diversification, and risk management.

By implementing these strategies, you can maximize your passive income potential and work towards achieving your financial goals.

Tips for accelerating your passive income growth

Accelerating your passive income growth requires dedication, discipline, and a willingness to take risks. Here are some tips to consider:

1. Focus on high-yield investments: High-yield investments, such as dividend-paying stocks or real estate properties with high rental yields, can generate more passive income than low-yield investments.

2. Reinvest your passive income: Reinvesting your passive income can accelerate your growth by compounding your returns over time. By reinvesting

your passive income, you can buy more shares or assets, which in turn generate more passive income.

3. Use leverage: Leverage can help you increase your returns by borrowing money to invest in high-yield assets, such as rental properties. However, leverage also comes with higher risk, so it's important to evaluate the potential risks and rewards before using it.

4. Focus on long-term growth: Passive income is a long-term strategy, and focusing on long-term growth rather than short-term gains can help you achieve greater success. Avoid chasing quick returns and instead focus on building a diversified portfolio that generates stable, sustainable income over time.

5. Stay disciplined and patient: Building passive income takes time and requires discipline and patience. Stick to your investment strategy, continue to reinvest your passive income, and be patient as your portfolio grows over time.

By implementing these tips, you can accelerate your passive income growth and work towards achieving your financial goals more quickly.

Ways to increase your returns through strategic reinvestment

Reinvesting your passive income is a powerful way to increase your returns and accelerate your passive income growth. Here are some ways to strategically reinvest your passive income:

1. Reinvest dividends and capital gains: If you're investing in stocks or funds, consider reinvesting your dividends and capital gains. This allows you to purchase more shares without incurring any additional costs, which can help you compound your returns over time.

2. Use dollar-cost averaging: Dollar-cost averaging involves investing a fixed amount of money at regular intervals, regardless of the current price of the asset. By using this strategy, you can buy more shares when prices are low and fewer shares when prices are high, which can help you maximize your returns over time.

3. Rebalance your portfolio: As your portfolio grows, it's important to rebalance your investments to maintain your desired asset allocation. This involves selling some assets and buying others to ensure that

your portfolio remains diversified and aligned with your investment strategy.

4. Consider tax-efficient investments: Tax-efficient investments, such as municipal bonds or index funds, can help you minimize your tax liability and increase your after-tax returns.

5. Invest in high-yield assets: Investing in high-yield assets, such as dividend-paying stocks or real estate properties with high rental yields, can help you generate more passive income and increase your overall returns.

By strategically reinvesting your passive income, you can accelerate your growth and work towards achieving your financial goals more quickly. However, it's important to evaluate the potential risks and rewards of each investment opportunity and to maintain a long-term investment strategy that aligns with your financial goals.

Balancing your passive income with your lifestyle goals

When building a passive income portfolio, it's important to balance your income goals with your lifestyle goals.

Here are some tips to help you achieve a balance between your passive income and your lifestyle:

1. Define your lifestyle goals: Before you start building your passive income portfolio, take the time to define your lifestyle goals. What kind of lifestyle do you want to lead? What are your priorities and values? By understanding your lifestyle goals, you can make investment decisions that align with your values and help you achieve the kind of life you want to live.

2. Set realistic income goals: Setting realistic income goals is important when building a passive income portfolio. Consider your lifestyle goals, financial needs, and risk tolerance when setting your income goals. It's important to remember that building a passive income portfolio takes time, so be patient and stay committed to your investment strategy.

3. Choose passive income streams that align with your values: When selecting passive income opportunities, choose investments that align with your values and priorities. For example, if you value sustainable living, consider investing in renewable energy projects. If you're passionate about social justice, consider investing in impact funds that support social and environmental causes.

4. Automate your passive income: Automating your passive income can help you achieve a better work-life balance. Set up automatic deposits into your investment accounts and automate your dividend reinvestment plan. This will help you avoid the temptation to constantly monitor your investments and allow you to focus on other areas of your life.

5. Re-evaluate your investment strategy regularly: As your lifestyle and financial goals change, it's important to re-evaluate your investment strategy regularly. Regularly reviewing and adjusting your portfolio can help you stay on track and achieve a better balance between your passive income and your lifestyle goals.

By balancing your passive income goals with your lifestyle goals, you can build a passive income portfolio that supports the kind of life you want to live. It's important to stay committed to your investment strategy and make adjustments as needed to ensure that your portfolio remains aligned with your values and priorities.

Achieving financial independence and retiring aggressively

Achieving financial independence and retiring aggressively is the ultimate goal for many people building a passive income portfolio. Here are some tips to help you achieve financial independence and retire aggressively:

1. Set a retirement goal: Setting a retirement goal is an important first step in achieving financial independence. Determine the amount of money you will need to live comfortably in retirement and use that as your goal. Consider factors such as your desired lifestyle, medical expenses, and travel plans.

2. Create a retirement plan: Once you have set a retirement goal, create a plan to achieve it. Determine how much you need to save each month and which passive income streams will help you reach your goal. Consider diversifying your portfolio to minimize risk.

3. Monitor your progress: Regularly monitor your progress towards your retirement goal. This will help you identify any issues or obstacles that may be hindering your progress. Adjust your investment strategy if needed to ensure that you are on track to achieve your retirement goal.

4. Consider retiring aggressively: Retiring aggressively means retiring earlier than the traditional retirement

age of 65. To retire aggressively, you will need to save more aggressively and invest in high-growth passive income opportunities. Consider investing in real estate, dividend-paying stocks, and other high-growth opportunities that can help you reach your retirement goal faster.

5. Be prepared for unexpected expenses: It's important to be prepared for unexpected expenses, such as medical bills or home repairs, when planning for retirement. Consider setting up an emergency fund to cover unexpected expenses

Achieving financial independence and retiring aggressively requires discipline, commitment, and a long-term investment strategy. By setting a retirement goal, creating a plan, monitoring your progress, and diversifying your portfolio, you can build a passive income portfolio that helps you achieve your retirement goals and live the life you want.

VIII. Conclusion

Passive income is a powerful tool for building wealth, achieving financial independence, and retiring aggressively. By understanding the different types of passive income streams available, evaluating your financial goals, assessing your resources, and diversifying your income streams, you can create a passive income portfolio that generates steady income and grows over time. Real estate investing, stock market investing, and alternative investments such as peer-to-peer lending and cryptocurrency can all be effective ways to build a passive income portfolio. By following the tips outlined in this book, you can maximize your passive income potential, accelerate your passive income growth, and achieve financial independence and retirement on your terms. Remember, building a passive income portfolio takes time, patience, and discipline, but the rewards can be significant. Start building your passive income portfolio today and take control of your financial future.